BAREFOOT ABE

BAREFOOT ABE

A REALLY TRULY STORY BY
SADYEBETH AND ANSON LOWITZ
WITH ILLUSTRATIONS BY THE LATTER

LERNER PUBLICATIONS COMPANY / MINNEAPOLIS, MINNESOTA

The Really Truly Stories

Barefoot Abe
The Cruise of Mr. Christopher Columbus
General George the Great
Mr. Key's Song
The Magic Fountain
The Pilgrims' Party
Tom Edison Finds Out

Third Printing 1969
Fourth Printing 1970
Fifth Printing 1972

Revised edition copyright © 1967 by Sadyebeth and Anson Lowitz

Original copyright 1938 by Sadyebeth and Anson Lowitz

International Standard Book Number: 0-8225-0135-X

Library of Congress Catalog Card Number: 67-29824

Manufactured in the United States of America

TO ROBERT DENY
and
TO THOSE
FOR WHOM
HE WAS NAMED

PUBLISHER'S NOTE: Over a generation ago the Really Truly Stories were widely acclaimed by critics throughout the country and hailed as classics in the field of children's literature. Many parents and librarians have remembered these wonderful books and asked to have them published again . . . and that is what has happened. We take great pride in presenting this LERNER EDITION OF A UNIQUE CLASSIC for the enjoyment of a new generation.

Years and years ago, when your grandfather's grandfather was a little boy, Thomas Lincoln and Nancy Hanks were married. Everyone for miles around came to the wedding supper. They knew there'd be lots to eat.

When the party was over, the Lincolns left on a horse.

They lived for awhile in a rented house, where baby Sarah was born. But Nancy wanted a home of her own, so Tom went out and built one.

It was made of logs, with one window and door. Hard packed earth was used for the floor. There was only one room where they worked, slept and ate. The Lincolns weren't much for style.

On February 12, 1809, a baby boy was born.   He was named Abraham, after his grandfather.   Of course, this name was much too big for such a tiny fellow.   They called him "Abe" instead.

He was homely and red and relatives said he'd never amount to much.

Tom Lincoln was a carpenter but work was hard to get. So, when Abe
was three, the family moved again.
It didn't take them long to pack. They hardly owned a thing.

Their new home was on a main road. Business was better there. Tom
made windows and doors, spinning wheels and chests of drawers.
He put them all together with little wooden pegs. Nails were scarce.

When Sarah and Abe were old enough, they sometimes went to school. This wasn't very often. For only traveling teachers came their way, and since they seldom got much pay, they didn't stay for long.

Books were few. There was usually only one. The teacher needed that. The children learned their lessons by saying them aloud, over and over again. It was hard for some to learn.

The streams around the Lincoln farm were simply crammed with fish.
Abe often caught a meal full.   But one day he fished and fished.
All he got was one.

On the way home he met an old soldier with a very hungry look.
Abe's mother had taught him to be extra kind to soldiers.   So he gave
the man his only fish.   It wasn't very big.

Abe never had much time to play.   There was always work to be done.
He took to the woods whenever he could.   There he had most of his fun.

Once he went for a little hike with another boy, named Austin.
Coming to a river, they started across on a slippery log.   In Abe fell!
First he kicked.   Then he splashed.   He couldn't swim a stroke.
Austin pulled him out with a stick.   Abe was wet clear through.

Another day, the boys set out, wearing their coon-skin hats.
Before very long they took them off to climb a pawpaw tree.
Abe was the first one up.   Below lay Austin's hat.

Quickly Abe dropped a pawpaw fruit.   It hit the hat—KER-SPLASH!
    Austin laughed and laughed.
He'd swapped Abe's hat for his when Abe had not been looking.

Tom Lincoln liked to move about.   New places sounded better.
Hearing how big things grew in Indiana, he couldn't wait to get there.
So he sold the farm and built himself a flatboat.

Then he loaded the boat with all it would hold, and set out alone to find a
    new place to call home.
Abe and his mother and sister came down to see him off.

Things went fine for quite a time.   Tom Lincoln took it easy.
The weather was good.   The river was smooth.   And he was in no hurry.
Suddenly, the boat bumped into a snag.   CRASH!!
Barrels, boxes, Thomas and all went in with a SPLASH!!

Tom Lincoln was very sad.   All he owned was at the bottom of the river.
It kept him pretty busy but he finally fished things out.

Tom stored what he'd saved with a couple of friends. Then he headed
straight for the woods. Finding a spot that looked good to him, he
chopped himself a clearing. Back he went for the family.
The Lincolns were glad to see him. They wanted to hear all the news.

Tom told such tales of his Indiana farm, they decided to leave at once.
Blankets and bundles, a bucket of fire and the family Bible were loaded on
a pair of borrowed horses. The Lincolns climbed on, too.

It was a long, long ride to Indiana, with hardly a road to guide them. They found their food along the way. They slept beneath the stars. At long last they came to the place Tom Lincoln had chosen.

When they got there, there was nothing but land. Mrs. Lincoln was rather surprised. Since it was just about time to get cold they built a three-sided shed. It wasn't much for comfort but there they stayed a year.

At the first sign of Spring, Tom Lincoln got to work, building a top-notch cabin.   The rest of the family helped.   They were used to it. Abe was only eight, but how he could swing an ax!

When the cabin was finished, the Lincolns just walked in.   They hadn't much to move.   They were proud of their new home.   It was the best they'd ever had.   Yet it had no window and no floor.   A hole in the wall was the only door.   Abe had a loft all his own.

Abe lived in this house for fourteen years.   He seldom got away.   A day in school meant a round-trip hike of nearly eighteen miles. The school was hardly worth it.

The path he took led through the woods, where the deer and the wildcats roamed.   Sometimes he heard a black bear growl. Sometimes he chased a fox to its hole.

Not long after their new home was built, Mrs. Lincoln died.
Life in the woods had been too hard for her.
The children missed her very much.   She'd always been so kind.

Sarah and Abe did their best to keep the household going.
There was far too much to do.
Abe carried corn to be ground at the mill, seven miles away.   Sarah did
    the sewing and cooking.   She was only eleven.   Abe was nine.

The Lincolns' meat came from the woods.   There were no butcher shops.
They ate partridge and grouse, rabbits and bear.   Often they had deer.
From deer they also got their clothes, the way the Indians did.   Deer skin
was good for shirts and pants, as well as moccasins.

One day a flock of wild turkeys went strutting past the cabin.
Abe grabbed his father's gun and aimed it through a crack.   BOOM!
There lay the biggest turkey.   Abe felt so bad he never shot another.

It seemed to Abe and Sarah that their work was never done. Wood Abe
   chopped was soon burned up.   Sarah's cooking was gone in a jiffy.
   Then it was time to chop and cook again.
Day after day Tom sat and thought.   At last he left home in a hurry.

Weeks later, a wagon   pulled up to the door.   Out Tom jumped.
He brought Abe and Sarah surprises galore—two sisters, a brother, a
   brand new mother and a houseful of furniture.

Abe's new mother was very nice.   He liked her right from the start.
She'd brought along all kinds of things he'd never seen before.
A feather bed, a clothes chest, a fine black walnut bureau.
Knives and forks and tablespoons, as well as pots and skillets.

Mrs. Lincoln took a look around.   Things were quite run down.
Abe's bed of leaves up in the loft just simply wouldn't do.
That night he slept on a feather bed for the first time in his life.

The new Mrs. Lincoln had ideas of her own about the comforts of home.
Knowing that Tom was a carpenter, she put him back to work.
First she asked for windows. Then she wanted a door. Next, she had
  him cutting planks for a wooden floor. Abe and his new brother helped.

In no time at all, the old log cabin wasn't what it used to be.

Meanwhile Abe just grew and grew.   Folks thought he'd never stop.
His arms grew long.   His sleeves grew short.   Nothing he owned ever fit.

By the time that he was seventeen he measured six feet four.

Abe was as strong as he was tall.   He could lift most anything.
When people needed something moved, they simply called on him.
One day he saw some men at work.   They were trying to lift a corn crib.
Abe picked it up and set it down right where they wanted it.

Another time he met two men about to move a chicken coop.
He quickly tossed it on his back and gave the hens a ride.

Abe hardly ever went to school but he tried his best to learn.
He borrowed books for miles around.   There weren't very many.
Josiah Crawford once loaned him a book about George Washington.
Abe promised to handle it with care.   That night it rained right through
the roof.   The book got wringing wet.

Abe pulled corn stalks two whole days so he could pay for it.

Most folks went to bed at night.   They had nowhere else to go.
Abe couldn't bear to waste the time.   He worked while others slept.

Stretched out before the fire, he'd read and write and figure.   He did
arithmetic with charcoal on a wooden shovel.   Things he wanted to
erase had to be scraped off.   The shovel grew quite thin.   Things he
wanted to remember, he wrote on shingles.   Paper was hard to get.

Tom wanted Abe to be a carpenter but Abe didn't care for the work.
Instead he did odd jobs for the neighbors. They paid him for it.
He carried water, built fires, cleaned houses and tended babies.
He plowed, sowed, reaped, mowed. He also chopped wood and split rails.

Everyone liked to have Abe around. He could tell such funny stories.
Alone in the woods, he'd stand on stumps and practice making speeches.
Even the animals listened.

Not far away from the Lincoln farm, the Ohio river flowed. Steamboats traveling up and down, went by every day. They always stopped at larger towns and usually in between.

Those who wanted to catch a boat had someone row them to it. Abe often picked up extra change taking people out.

One day he helped two strangers board a boat they'd almost missed. They were so pleased, they each tossed him a shiny fifty cents. One fell in!

Abe hunted and hunted. He searched and searched. He fished and fished. Indeed, he tried so hard to find the money he nearly fell in, too. All he did was muddy up the water.

Anyway, money Abe earned wasn't his for keeps. His father took every last cent. Fathers used to do that till their sons were twenty-one. There were no allowances then.

Abe was known to everyone along the river front. He could handle a boat like a sailor. When he was nineteen, a Mr. Gentry asked him to pilot a flatboat to New Orleans. It was one thousand miles away. Abe thought the trip might do him good. He said he'd start at once.

Alas! Alack! There was no boat. Abe found he had to build it. Young Allan Gentry helped. He planned on going, too. When it was done, the boys set out with a load of food and things.

They sailed down the Ohio as far as it went.   Then the Mississippi.
It was a dangerous trip.   The rivers were brimful of bends and turns, sand
   bars, islands and fallen trees.   It was hard to make much time.
The two boys sailed from dawn till dark.   Nights, they tied up near shore.

One night, after supper, they turned in early.   They'd had a busy day.
Suddenly, Abe woke up with a jump.   River thieves were on their boat,
   about to help themselves.   The boys pushed them off in a hurry.

At New Orleans they sold the boat and everything they'd brought.
Then, after a quick sightseeing tour, they took a steamer home.

Abe talked so much about all he'd seen Tom Lincoln got quite restless.
He thought they'd better move on.   This time to Illinois.
As soon as they could, they sold their farm and bought a pair of oxen.
Then, with all they owned and thirteen relatives, the Lincolns headed West.
Abe sold pins and needles, buttons and suspenders, all along the way.

Now that Abe was twenty-one, he could keep whatever he earned. But he didn't always get money. People were short of that.
Anyway, he didn't care. He needed lots of things. All he owned was a faded shirt and some shrunken buckskin trousers.

He bargained once with Nancy Miller to make him a new pair of pants.
He said he'd split four hundred rails for every yard of cloth.
Abe's legs were long. When the pants were done they'd cost 1400 rails.

As soon as folks in Illinois saw that Abe was willing to work, they kept him much too busy. He turned down jobs every day.

However, when Mr. Offut asked him to take a flatboat to New Orleans, he accepted with thanks. He wanted another look at the city.

This time Abe saw the town, from one end to the other. He visited the market where slaves were bought and sold. It made him very sad. He promised himself, right then and there, that some day he would stop it.

Abe got home just in time to help with the moving again.
Then he left by canoe for New Salem to work in Offut's new store.
When he got there nothing was ready.   None of the goods had come.
In fact, there wasn't even a building.   Abe had to help put one up.

Offut's store kept all sorts of things.   Salt, sugar, shoes and socks.
Bonnets, butter, tea and hardware.   Molasses, gloves, tobacco and eggs.

Both Abe and Offut's other clerk slept in the store on a narrow cot.
Unless the boys turned over together, one was sure to fall out.

Abe was so very honest folks all called him "Honest Abe."   He seldom
   ever charged too much and tried to give full measure.
One day a lady bought some tea.   Offut's had the best.   When she'd gone
   Abe found he'd weighed it wrong.   He took her the other quarter
   pound when work was done that night.   It was a long, long walk.

Abe knew he had a lot to learn about the things in books.   Whenever he
could he dropped in at school and sat in the back of the room.
At first the children laughed and laughed.   Abe was twenty-three.

Teacher Graham was very kind.   He did what he could for Abe.
He was always glad to help him with Geography and Grammar.

Men often came to Offut's, just to sit and talk.   They seldom bought.
They'd brag and boast about themselves and all that they could do.
Mr. Offut liked to have them come.   He could boast with the very best.
One day he bragged that Abe could beat anyone he fought.

Now the Clary Grove boys were extra tough.   Jack Armstrong, the tough-
    est.   When he heard of Offut's boast, he picked a fight with Abe.
Abe beat him up completely and offered to fight the rest.   Off they ran!

Sometimes strangers passed the store on their way out West. They
usually stopped to chat a bit and buy a thing or two.
Once some travelers left behind a barrel full of trash.
There among old boots and junk Abe found a tattered law book.

He read it by day.   He read it by night.   He learned it all by heart.
He thought of lots and lots of things there ought to be laws against.
So he decided to run for the Legislature.   That's where laws were made.

Meanwhile, nearby Indians had started up a war. They'd sold their
hunting ground to the white men. Now they wanted it back.
The Governor asked for soldiers. Abe said he'd like to be one.

He climbed into his fighting togs and left with some of his friends.
Since Abe was by far the best fighter, they chose him captain. This
pleased him very much. But before they got to the war it was over.
Abe never fired a shot.

Home he hurried in a borrowed canoe.　It was time for people to vote.
They wanted someone honest and fair to help make laws for the State.

Abe made speeches everywhere.　But he didn't make quite enough.
Someone else was elected.　Abe could have used more friends.
Back he went to storekeeping, this time for himself.

Abe had a partner in the store.   Berry was his name.   He never was much
    help.   In a few months he disappeared, leaving the bills behind him.
The store had to close up right away but Abe paid back every cent.
It took him years and years.

Abe looked around for work to do.   Surveyors all seemed busy.   Illinois
    was new.   Every farm needed measuring.   In six weeks he learned how.

While measuring land Abe got about.   He made a lot of friends.   They liked his maps.   They liked his jokes.   They thought him very smart. When New Salem needed a Postmaster, Abe was asked to take the job. He said he'd be delighted, if he could keep on with his regular work.

Every day, on his way to survey, he'd stop to deliver the mail.   He carried the letters in the crown of his hat.   There weren't very many.

Abe went on studying law.   He still wanted that job with the State.
When election time came round again, he called on all his friends.
He needed every vote.

He made speeches by the dozen.   He called at farms for miles around.
Once he asked some workers in a field to vote for him.
They said they'd vote for anyone who could beat them cutting grain.
Abe took off his coat and went to work and led them around the field.

This time Abe won the election.   He started right in making laws.
The work was pretty easy.   He was a lawyer now.

While Abe was in the Legislature, it was moved to Springfield. · Abe
  moved, too.   Moving wasn't new to him.
He rode into town on a borrowed horse.   One bag held all he owned.

The job with the State didn't take all his time.   In between, Abe was a lawyer.   Folks who'd gotten into trouble hired him to get them out. Now, at that time, judges and lawyers rode from place to place.   Towns didn't have their own.   Abe often went along.   One day he stopped to put two baby birds back into their nest.   He believed in being kind. The other lawyers laughed.

Nights, they'd tell stories round a fire.   Abe always knew the best.

The tavern where Abe lived awhile was kept by Mr. Rutledge.   He had a
    daughter, Ann.   Abe liked her very much.
When she died, quite suddenly, he was very sad.

Some years later, he met Mary Todd.   She was plump and pretty and
    she'd been to school a lot.   Her father was a banker and very well-to-do.
It took Abe a long time to make up his mind but at last he married her.
They went to live at Globe Tavern.   Here baby Robert was born.

The Lincolns soon found that they needed more room. So they bought a little house. There baby Edward was born.

That same year Abe was asked to go to Congress to help make laws for the country. Mrs. Lincoln was delighted. She began to pack at once.

The Lincolns arrived in Washington, all dressed up in their Sunday best. Folks called Abe "Mr. Lincoln" now.

In those days, our country was growing.   States were being added all the
time.   Stephen Douglas wanted to allow slaves in the new States.
Mr. Lincoln didn't.   He longed to be a Senator.   Then he'd try to stop it.

However, Mr. Douglas had that job and thought he'd like to keep it.
So short Mr. Douglas and tall Mr. Lincoln went around together making
speeches.   Both had reasons all their own why they should be elected.

Mr. Lincoln talked his best.   Mr. Douglas, even better.   He'd had more
    practice.   When every vote was counted Mr. Douglas had the most.
Mr. Lincoln was disappointed.   But not for long.   The country needed a
    new President and he was asked to try out for the job.

Some of the country's great men came to the house to deliver the invita-
    tion.   They were met at the gate by Willie and Tad, Lincoln's young-
    est sons.   The boys said to go on in.   Their father'd be right down.

Mr. Lincoln was most surprised. He accepted with thanks. Then, as soon as he could, he set out to get votes. It kept him pretty busy. Once a little girl wrote she'd help get votes if he'd let his whiskers grow. He wrote to say he might—some day. Then he grew a chin full.

When the votes were counted Mr. Lincoln had the most. Back he came to Washington. As he rode through town the people cheered and cheered. He was President Lincoln now.

But, alas! Soon there was trouble everywhere. The Southern States decided to choose their own President and start another country. The Northern States said they couldn't. So war began between the States.

President Lincoln was most upset. He wanted the United States to be one country. But, try as he did, it took four years to get it together again. Before the war was over, he kept a promise he'd once made. He signed a big, long paper which said the slaves were free.

President Lincoln had little time to play.   There was always work to do.
But it didn't matter what it was, he'd stop if Tad came in.
Together they'd play with toy soldiers.   They'd joke and laugh and read.
Whenever Tad did something bad and his father had to scold, he'd
always try to fix things up.   Somehow, he seemed to understand.

Then he'd take Tad on his knee and tell him about another little boy
who once had wandered barefoot through the woods.